BETWEEN SHADOWS AND LIGHT

POEMS ON LOVE, FATE, AND THE INFINITE

THE IMPULSIVE POETS

For my mother,
whose absence became the silence
that taught me how to write.

I started when I lost you.
And somehow, every word still feels like
a way back to you.

Contents

Contents

Foreword

I never intended to become a poet.

But grief has a way of pulling language from the depths of your silence.

I was just a boy when I lost my mother. The world felt too big, too hollow—and I had no idea what to do with the ache. So I started writing. First in fragments. Then in verses. Eventually, poetry became the only way I could keep breathing without being crushed by the weight of it all.

Between Shadows and Light is not just a book of poems. It's a mirror of everything I've wrestled with: love that didn't last, dreams that almost died, nights I couldn't sleep, and the fire that kept me moving anyway. Each piece is a glimpse into my contradictions—how I burn with rebellion but still crave tenderness, how I lose myself in longing but somehow keep finding clarity in the chaos.

Some of these poems were written in one breath. Others sat with me for months. All of them are honest.

If you've ever felt too much, this book is for you. If you've ever stood at the edge of something—grief, love, fate, or your own reflection—I hope you find a piece of yourself in these pages.

Thank you for reading.

Thank you for feeling.

— The Impulsive Poets

Preface

This collection wasn't built in a rush.

It came together like life does—fragment by fragment, in moments both burning and quiet.

I didn't set out with a structure in mind. I simply wrote when something inside me moved—when I couldn't sleep, when a memory haunted me, when love felt too close or too far. Over the years, these poems piled up like echoes of my inner world. I began to notice themes: rebellion and surrender, desire and distance, the way fate keeps us tethered even when we fight it.

That's how Between Shadows and Light found its form.

Four chapters. One journey.

The Fire Within captures rebellion, passion, and the urge to break free.

Between Love and Longing holds the ache of closeness and the silence that follows.

Light and Shadow explores the fragile line between strength and sorrow.

The Threads of Fate dives about existence, purpose, and the infinite.

I haven't edited these poems to perfection. I've kept them close to how they first arrived—raw, real, and rooted in the moment. Because that's what life feels like. Not perfect. Just true.

I hope you read these not just as poems, but as pages from a life lived between extremes.

Thank you for stepping into the space between shadows and light with me.

— The Impulsive Poets

Prologue

Before the words came, there was silence.

Not peace—just the heavy quiet of things unsaid.

    I didn't know what I was searching for.

Only that something inside me refused to stay still.

Loss cracked me open.

Longing gave me rhythm.

And love—

love taught me how to speak with my eyes closed.

    This book is not a roadmap.

It's a storm. A kiss. A confession left behind in the margins.

It's everything I couldn't tell the world,

so I told the page.

    If you've ever lived between the lines,

welcome home.

Acknowledgements

To everyone who's ever made me feel deeply—thank you.

Some of you loved me.

Some of you hurt me.

Some of you simply passed through, unaware you left footprints behind.

Each of you gave me a line, a scar, or a reason to write.

To my mother—this book was born the day I lost you.

Your absence became the space where all my words began.

You are the shadow and the light in everything I do.

To the ones who kept showing up when I didn't have the words—

thank you for holding space, for asking how I was even when I stayed silent.

To every artist, poet, and wild soul I've drawn inspiration from—

especially Pablo Neruda—for showing me that poetry doesn't just describe life, it dares to feel it.

And to you, the reader—

Thank you for opening this book. For feeling what I felt.

These pages are no longer just mine. They're yours now too.

—The Impulsive Poets

1. Chapter 1: The Fire Within (Rebellion, Passion, and The Urge to Break Free.)

Strip Me Down

lying on the lowly settled dust over a hill

and watching those barn owls cruising past the dusky sun

I had thoughts crossing over my mind

no matter what I feel 'right' from the heart

is never 'right' for the camaraderie

it is a state of extreme feebleness

and who's to decide what's right?

some days I'm so suffocated from this complex world

that

I want to strip my tie

tear my clothes

I just want to free myself from 'me'

all I want to do is to escape the camaraderie

break the chains

run so hard

that

all I can feel would be the pain of my knees

and nothing else

I want to wander in the wild untamed

play in the dirt

dance in the rain

soil my clothes

just jump into the river

and once I'm tired

want to grab the soiled fruits from the earth

want to live by my own terms

don't wanna be organized'

and I promise I hate the straight roads

I really don't know if I'm allowed to say this

but every time I cannot follow my heart

I feel like I lose a part of me

deep down my heart I know

there's somewhere in this world

where there's air of liberty

Is the battle of life to be the true you?

or

to be the one in this aristocratic society?

For You

I love you for simply being you,

a soul so radiant, inside and out.

I'm drawn to the way you care—

for your people, for the world, for me.

I cherish our conversations,

the ones where dreams take flight,

where life unfolds between our words,

and the future feels within reach.

I love the way your eyes find me,

soft, warm, brimming with love.

The way your kisses hold meaning,

each one a whisper of affection.

But beyond it all, I love your essence—

the way you move through life,

spreading light when your heart is free.

Your

utterly beauteous soul,

selfless kindness,

and that infectious smile—

make me long to taste the softness of your lips.

The Reign and the Fall

The tiresome breaths began to fade,

after the playful, innocent melee.

We lay side by side, dropped low, exhausted.

Her hand, so soft, brushed against mine.

I turned towards her, eyes tracing curves,

a fleeting glance before I seized her wrist.

She felt my grasp—

I felt her breath, rising,

falling, like the tide beneath my touch.

I saw her battle her will,

kissed her tresses, slid down to her ear,

whispered with a bite—

she froze.

A pause, a pulse,

her heartbeat echoed in the hush of the room.

She sighed, then rose,

gathered her fire,

legs entwining, claiming her reign.

Pinned beneath her,

I watched her strength unfold,

hands locked behind my head,

her defiance a fleeting flame.

She fought for control—

I let her have it, let her feel it,

as she held me prisoner beneath her skin.

But the struggle was fleeting.

The reign was short.

She knew.

I knew.

Her lips hovered, teasing, but never touching,

until I shattered her hold.

Turned the tides,

wrapped her in my grasp,

breathed her in,

felt the tremble in her spine.

She knew her reign was long.

She knew her reign was over.

And in one swift motion—

she surrendered.

Hooked Up

The taste of you still lingers,

like the last drag of a cigarette—

sharp, intoxicating, impossible to forget.

Your voice, a whisper in the wind,

echoing in the hollow spaces of my mind.

I tell myself it's just a memory,

but memories don't burn this deep.

Your hands,

they once unraveled me,

pulled me closer,

only to leave me tangled in your absence.

Nights pass, yet the phantom of your touch

still presses against my skin.

I try to let go—

but the past tightens like a noose.

I light another cigarette,

watch the smoke curl and fade.

If only forgetting you

was as easy as watching something disappear.

2. Chapter 2: Between Love and Longing (Connection, Devotion, and the Spaces in Between)

Unwind

As he followed me with an immense ease,

Watching my hips sway around me,

And the light just enough

To highlight my curves.

Keeping up the pace,

And unable to control the yearning,

He grabbed my waist and pushed me against the wall.

I tried to get rid of the muscular hold,

Although not so angry, for I knew this was coming.

Taking in my scent, which was probably too much to handle,

Tightening his hold,

He dug his head into my seemingly delicious neck

And sucked upon it earnestly.

Softening my push, I closed my eyes and moaned,

Savoring the arousal.

He trailed down my body, encircling the nipple

Which had grown even harder,

My navel never settling,

Making me covet even more.

I clawed his hair and bit his ear,

I could feel the jolt rising within him.

Unhesitantly, he slid his hand under my skirt

And tiptoed over my thighs to the silk between my legs.

I straddled, wanting him there,

Shivering vehemently in the cold breeze.

Having done its job,

The moon pulled the curtain over itself.

The Interwoven Paths

We walk,

each step unknowingly guided by echoes

of roads we never took.

Threads unseen, yet tightly wound,

binding us to choices made

long before we had a say.

A glance, a missed moment,

a word left unsaid—

tiny ripples in the vast ocean of time,

pulling us toward fates

we once thought were our own making.

Were we ever truly free,

or are we merely wanderers

along paths interwoven long before

we even learned to walk?

Perhaps it is not about the roads we take,

but the footprints we leave behind—

the fleeting marks of our existence

on a world that forgets too soon.

The Unspoken

You speak without words,

your eyes tracing every unguarded thought

etched in the quiet between us.

I feel your presence linger,

like a melody left unfinished,

a song that only we can hear.

The weight of the unsaid

settles between our breaths,

heavy, yet impossibly light.

Do you know?

Do you feel it too?

The way silence hums with longing,

the way absence still holds your shape.

Some things are never spoken,

yet they are heard all the same.

10 Lines

If I could paint the sky with your name, I would.

If I could bottle your laughter, I'd drink it forever.

If time stood still in your arms, I'd never move.

If distance called, I'd whisper, "Not today."

If love had a face, it would look like you.

If silence could speak, it would echo your voice.

If longing had hands, it would reach for you.

If dreams were real, I'd wake up beside you.

If forever was a choice, I'd choose you twice.

If I never said it—know that I always meant to.

In Silence You Stay

Sometimes,

Very sometimes in life,

talking to the right person feels like a quiet melody.

You know every word leaving their lips

is something you've longed to hear.

You watch them talk,

shy away with that sigh of happiness,

cherishing the wait like it's a moment worth living for.

And when you finally see them,

all you want to do is drown in their serene eyes,

trace your hands along their waist,

and kiss them—

like it's the last time the world allows you to.

Even when they're not around, they are.

A thousand thoughts, a thousand times.

And when sleep finally takes you,

you know they're with you.

In silence, you drift,

wearing that innocent smile you never even noticed.

Never Say Goodbye

I totally understand everything you said,

And I'm glad you broke the silence.

I know the importance of space,

And I respect your decision.

But it's hard to accept,

And I can't begin to fathom what's in your mind.

You are a part of me,

And I don't know how to let that go.

I wish I had said all this

While you were still in front of me.

I respect you more than words can hold,

And I know you'll always be that same incredible person.

I've realized—staying in touch doesn't matter,

Because you will always be here, within me.

Never forget, I'm just a letter away,

And I will never say goodbye.

3. Chapter 3: Light and Shadow (The Interplay of Joy and Sorrow, Strength and Fragility)

Hooked Up

There is this part of me which is still anchored at the memories we
have made.

I scream to drop the hook

But believe me

it gets stouter each fuckin time.

I have been so foolhardy all my life

in making even the cardinal decisions

which paved the path

to the life I'm living right now

but

this decision to choose a life

with or without you

is harder than I ever thought.

You know what's ceasing me to drop the hook?

It's that slight hint of hope

Which is cooking from the pot

that things were great in the past

and it could be great in the future too.

Should I jump into a cascade, the same uncertain life I was living?

Or Should I live with the unfamiliar certainty?

Chasing the Light

When I close my eyes for a moment,

I see the inner me—closer than ever.

Fear creeps in, the world shatters,

The air is thick, the night is endless.

A silent whisper crawls through the dark,

A past I once called fate—

Now just fragments waiting to be mended.

The weight of it all, pulling me in,

But I keep moving, step by step.

Each day, a battle within,

Shadows stretching, testing my will.

The closer I get, the heavier it feels,

But I know—I have to see it through.

The city hums in the background,

Stories etched in midnight echoes.

Broken pieces scattered in the quiet,

Each one telling me who I was, who I am.

Eyes shut, I listen to the silence,

Let it drown the noise, strip me bare.

And in that moment—just for a second,

I see the light breaking through.

Echoes of the Night

I run toward the flicker on the horizon,

A shimmer just beyond my grasp.

Each step forward, shadows stretch behind me,

Ghosts of moments I cannot outlast.

The night whispers doubts I pretend not to hear,

Yet the stars remind me—

Even in darkness, light lingers near.

I've stumbled through storms,

Lost my way in the quiet abyss,

But every fall has taught me—

The dawn is never far from this.

So I chase the light, though it dances away,

Not knowing if I will ever arrive.

But in the pursuit, I have found something greater—

The will to rise, the strength to survive.

Born into Light and Shade

We arrive, blinking, into the glow,

soft hands grasping at the weight of the world.

Cocooned in warmth, yet shadow lingers,

etched in the lines of a fate untold.

Day and night weave through our veins,

a silent rhythm we learn to obey.

Joy and sorrow, entwined from birth,

dancing in the spaces where light gives way.

Laughter echoes, sharp as pain,

love blooms even where endings stay.

No soul untouched by shadow's brush,

no heart immune to fleeting days.

Yet still, we walk, heads turned to the sun,

knowing the dark will always call.

For only in shade does light burn brighter,

and only in falling do we rise at all.

Selfless

For the hardships you have endured to nurture us,

for the hours you have worked without rest,

for the moments your thoughts revolved around us,

for the sleepless nights spent watching over us.

For the tears you have shed in silence,

for the sacrifices made without expectation,

for the love given without condition—

a love that asked for nothing in return.

We could never repay you,

never measure the depth of what you've given.

All we can offer is gratitude,

though even that feels too small.

4. Chapter 4: The Threads of Fate (Existence, Purpose, and the Infinite)

Intentions

unforged my intentions come beneath

when I'm holding you tight in my arms

feeling the present

amidst the chaos

is what you make me feel

entwined the cold breeze binding me,

making me want to kiss you even more

befuddling my mind

still lying to capture the vibration holding me in

exuberant you talking about things around you

makes me fail to recall this world

melting gently with ease my heart grows fonder

with every memory you create

can see the you within you

within you every moment

A Thread in Time

Woven into the fabric of moments,

I drift between what was and what will be.

A speck in the grand loom of existence,

tangled in patterns I cannot see.

I have lived lifetimes in passing thoughts,

died a thousand deaths in forgotten dreams.

Yet here I stand, still unfinished,

caught between meaning and the in-between.

The universe does not know my name,

nor does it care for the weight of my past.

But within me, a fire still lingers,

burning for a truth that will always outlast.

Never Feeling Alone

The imperturbable pacifying breeze

Swirling around

The upbeat alluring light

Glowing up

The innocent aroma of the damp soil

Constructing over

The elegant gaze of the blossoming floret

The stoned still pebbles nothing much serener

The boisterous shore frolicking around

The fine sand caressing my feet

The enigmatic horizon over my crown

Beneath the fervent abysmal blue sky

Living a world drenched in my imagination

But never feeling alone.

Never feeling alone.

A Speck in Infinite

Beneath the vast and endless sky,

I stand, a whisper in the grand design.

A fleeting breath, a flickering light,

A speck dissolving into time.

I watch the heavens stretch afar,

Galaxies swirl, oblivious to my name.

Yet here I am, pulsing, alive,

A witness to this fleeting game.

We carve our paths in dust and stone,

Build our stories, chase the sun.

We love, we lose, we rise, we fall,

Yet in the end, we're everyone.

No weight remains, no chains persist,

Just echoes of the lives we weave.

We come, we feel, we burn, we fade,

With nothing left to grieve.

So let me love without restraint,

And live with fire, unconfined.

For though I am but passing dust,

I am the dust that dared to shine.

Seeking

For even as the tides erase my steps,

I have left my weight upon the sand.

Not for the world to remember,

but for me to know I was here.

Fresh balmy air smoking under the mischievous juvenile sky

Deep enigmatic clouds of emotion

Entangled around my soul stronger than ever

Subtly wrecking my solemn assurance

light within me broke into a thousand hues

The unavoidable nothingness when you aren't around me

Still feels like you are right in my arms.

Closing Words

We are all walking contradictions—

aching and healing, loving and losing, burning and blooming.

I wrote these poems to make sense of that.

If they touched you,

even for a moment,

then maybe we've both found a little more light.

—The Impulsive Poets

Follow The Journey

Instagram: @theimpulsivepoets

Spotify / Apple Music: The Impulsive Poets

Email: theimpulsivepoets@gmail.com

Copyright